CW01216422

Published in 2015 by
North Parade Publishing Ltd.

All rights reserved

© North Parade Publishing Ltd.
4 North Parade
Bath
BA1 1LF
UK

My Book of 1000 Words

My Book of 1000 Words is the perfect introduction for children to the exciting and informative world of learning. This book is an essential vocabulary building tool for young children and early readers, and is designed to develop first reading and spelling skills. The book will enchant and stimulate young minds.

Children will love turning the pages to discover familiar concepts, objects, animals, activities, occupations and more. Each photograph is accompanied by a simple, easy-to-read caption. Designed to educate and entertain, this book will help children expand their vocabulary, improve word recognition skills and understand simple themes.

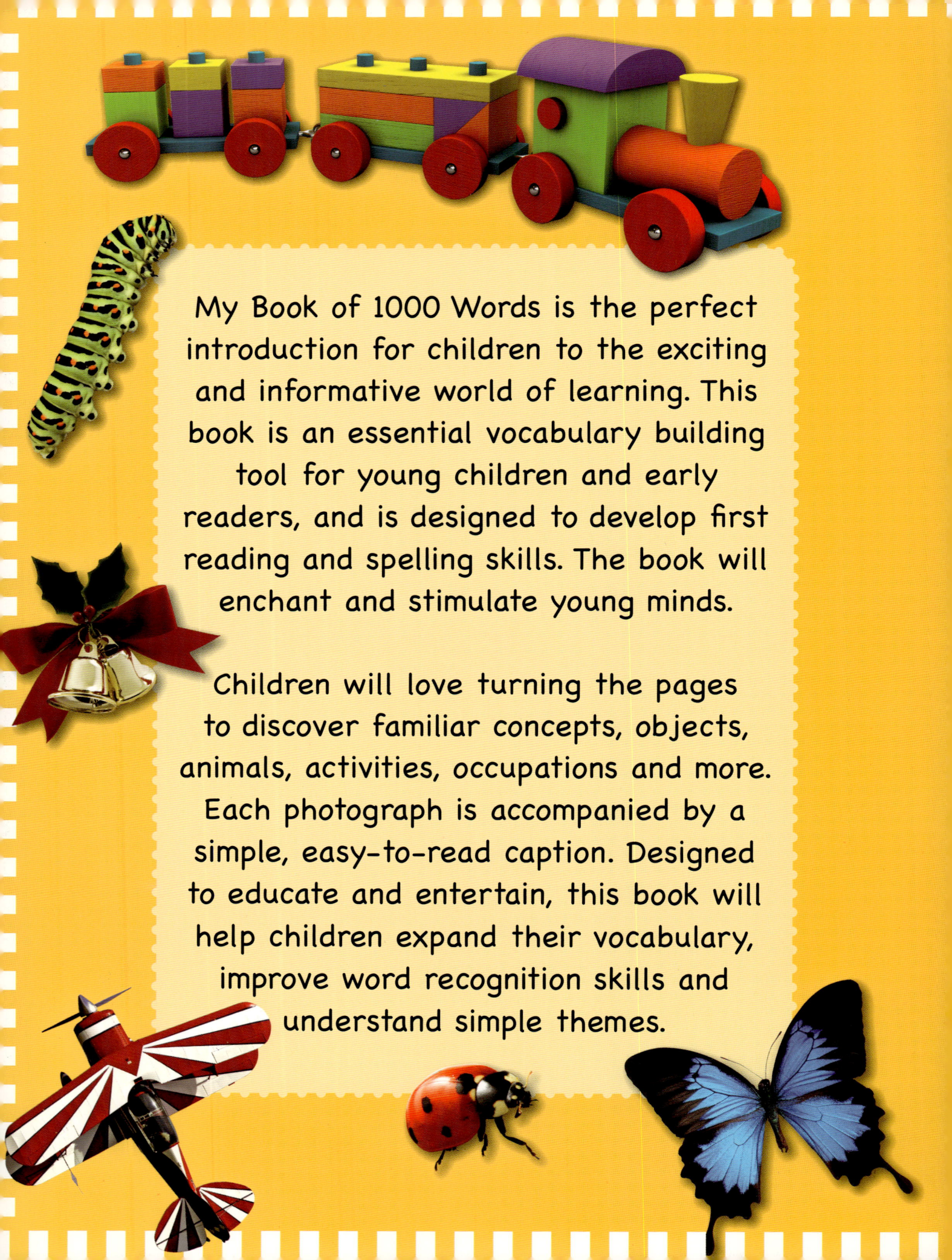

My Book of 1000 Words has been created as an essential early reference tool for preschoolers to help develop language skills, such as letter and word recognition. Playing sports and music, eating food, spending time at home – these common activities are entertainingly presented in colourful scenes with every key object labelled.

This fun-filled reference book introduces children to familiar words in the context of everyday situations. It's an ideal learning tool for home or classroom, providing hours of independent reading pleasure with family and friends.

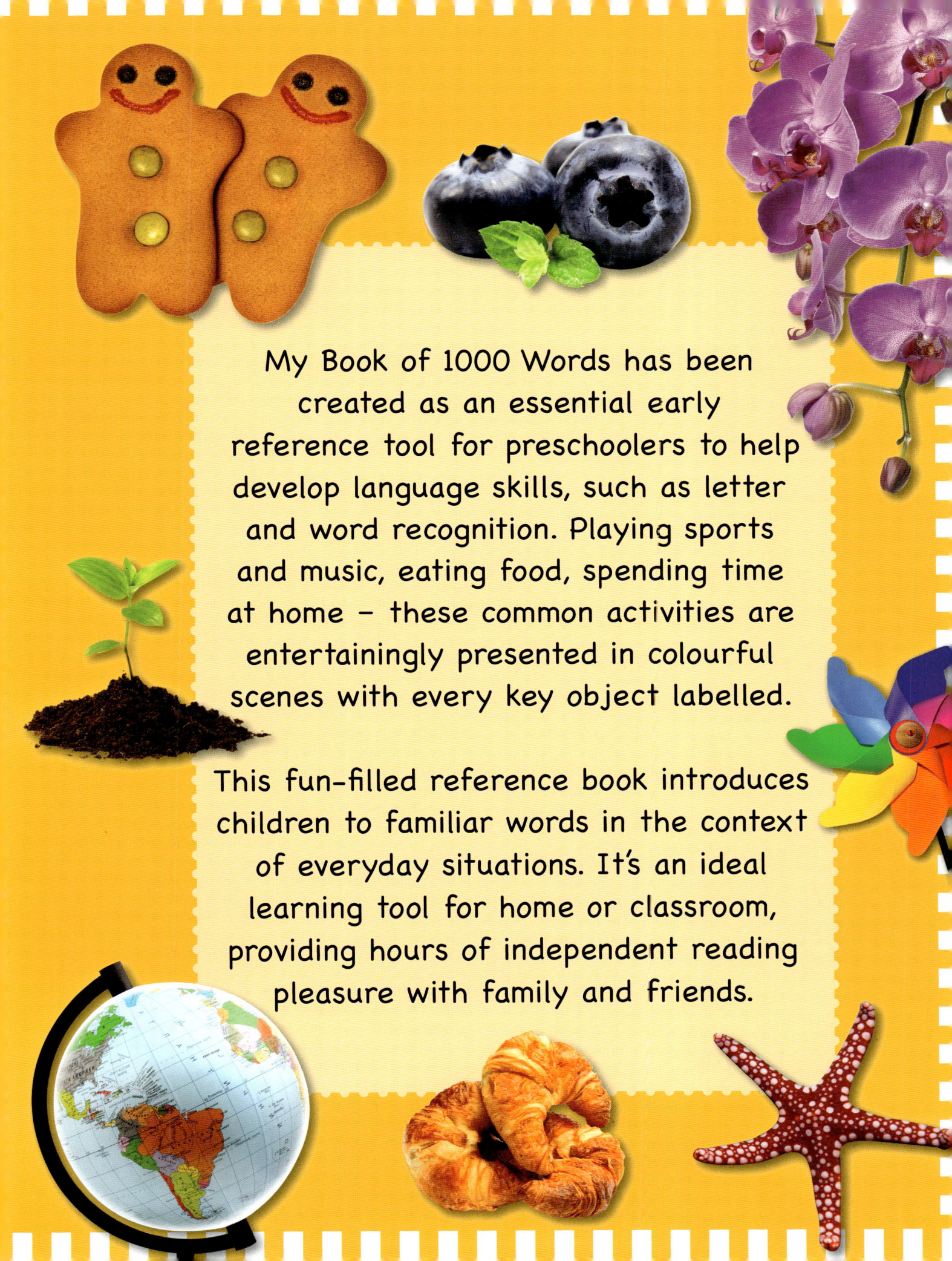

Household pets

These animals are found at home. Do you have any pets?

Goldfish

Budgerigar

Dog

Rabbit

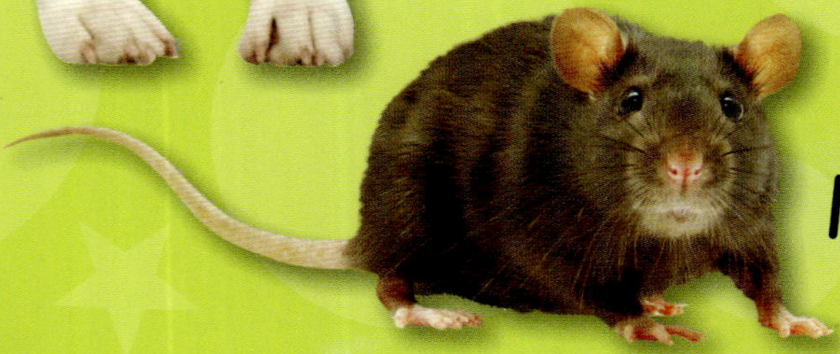

Mouse

Parrot

Lizard

Cat

Farm animals

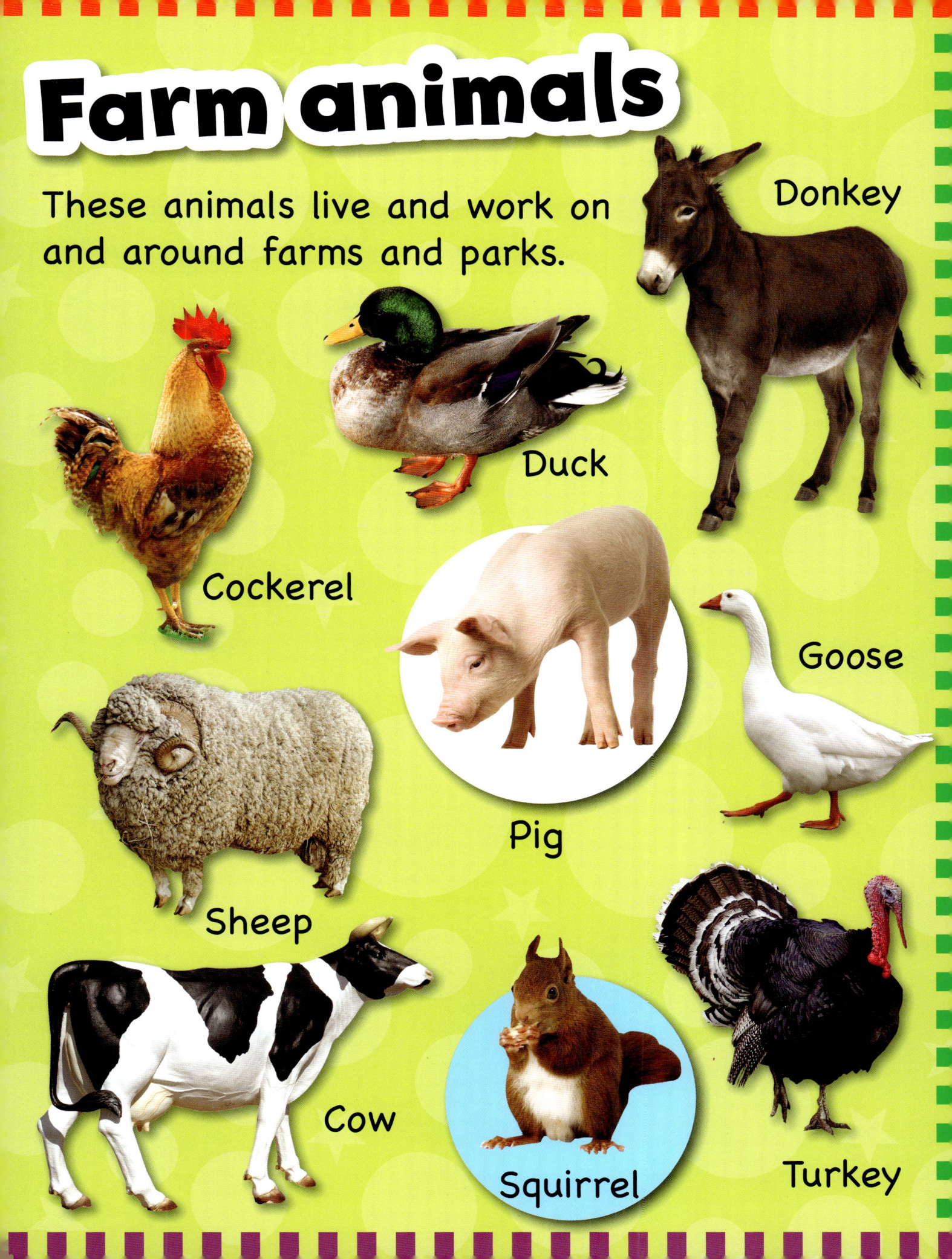

These animals live and work on and around farms and parks.

Donkey

Duck

Cockerel

Pig

Goose

Sheep

Cow

Squirrel

Turkey

In the garden

How many of these creatures have you seen in your garden?

Butterfly

Spider

Ant

Caterpillar

Starling

Robin

Bee

Ladybird

Centipede

Wasp

Moth

Snail

Grasshopper

Slug

Magpie

Green Cricket

Earthworm

In the jungle

These are some of the wild animals that live in or near jungles.

Snake

Hawk

Wolf

Tiger

Chimpanzee

Quetzal

Sloth Bear

Monkey

Toucan

Spider Monkey

Bat

Orangutan

Macaw

Warthog

Capybara

Howler Monkey

Leopard

On the grasslands

Some animals live on the grasslands. Let's take a look at them.

Wildebeest

Lion

Baboon

Impala

Giraffe

Zebra

Rhinoceros

Hyena

In the mountains

The mountains are also home to several animals. Let's see what they are.

- Addax
- Mountain Goat
- Ground Squirrel
- Brown Bear
- Panda
- Bison
- Snow Leopard
- Golden Eagle
- Gorilla

In the pond

Have you looked into a pond? Did you see any of these creatures?

Frog

Dragon Fly

Tadpole

Mosquito

Koi Carp

Salamander

Caddis Fly

Water Boatman

Toad

In the deserts

Animals can also be found in the deserts. Here are some of them.

Rattlesnake

Coyote

Ostrich

Dingo

Camel

Black Widow Spider

Vulture

Kangaroo

In the seas

The seas are home to many creatures as well as fish.

Dolphin

Sponge

Angel Fish

Star Fish

Sting Ray

Coral

Pelican

Parrot Fish

Killer Whale

Humpback Whale

Blue Tang

Seahorse

Gull

Eel

Crab

Octopus

Great White Shark

In the rivers

Even the rivers are teeming with wildlife and not all of them are fish.

River Turtle

Aligator

Boutu

Otter

Trout

Piranha

Anaconda

River Dolphin

At the poles

These creatures live in the extreme cold of the poles.

Penguin

Snow Owl

Arctic Fox

Walrus

Arctic Hare

Narwhal

Puffin

Seal

Polar Bear

Good morning

What do you do when you get up in the morning?

Toothbrush

Milk

Toothpaste

Cereal

Juice

Sugar

Spoon

Bread

Bowl

Eggs

Time for a bath

After brushing your teeth and having breakfast, it's time for a bath.

Towel

Bath Toy

Shampoo

Soap

Comb

Bathrobe

Bathtub

My body

These are the different important parts of your body.

Cheek

Tongue

Mouth

Lips

Stomach

Head

Legs

Nails

- Feet
- Hair
- Toes
- Eye
- Fingers
- Nose
- Teeth
- Arm
- Ear

What I do

How many of these activities do you do everyday?

Drink

Jump

Read

Play

Smile

Cry

Eat

Sleep

My clothes

These are the different types of clothes you wear everyday.

Gloves

Jacket

Shoes

Scarf

Socks

T-Shirt

Hat

Trousers

Sweater

Around the house

These are some objects around the house. Can you name them?

Chair

Television

Door

Vacuum

Lamp

Phone

Table

Radio

Key

Window

Music Player

Sofa

Fan

Air Conditioner

Egg Timer

Roof

Picture

Cushion

Washing Machine

DVD Player

Light Bulb

Plunger

Mop

Broom

Electric Socket

- Laundry Basket
- Ironing Board
- Detergent Bottle
- Lock
- Shaver
- Wall Switch
- Electric Iron
- Vase
- Bathroom Brush

- Kennel
- Birdhouse
- Fire Extinguisher
- Coaster
- Umbrella Stand
- Toolbox
- Rolodex

- Candelabra
- Coathanger
- Letterbox
- First aid box
- Curtain
- Stepladder
- Stool
- Fish Bowl
- Laundry Basket
- Bathmat

Its bedtime

It's time for bed. Do you recognise these objects?

Pillow

Bed

Pyjamas

Blanket

Soft Toy

Night Light

Books

Reading Lamp

Colours

How many of these colours do you recognise?

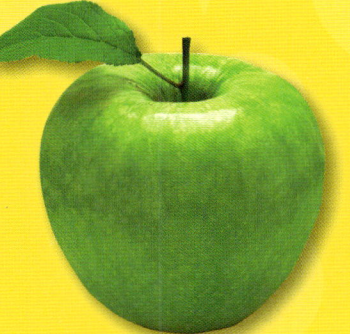

Green Apple

Orange

Violet Flower

Yellow Flower

Red Purse

Black Hat

Blue Butterfly

Grey Bag

Purple Aubergine

Let's play

Which of these toys would you like to play with?

Toy Train

Rattle

Tricycle

Monkey

Pinwheel

Guitar

Truck

Toy Plane

Robot

Ball

Toy Phone

Toy Blocks

Wagon

Rocking Horse

Doll

Car

Getting ready

Going on a trip? Let's get ready for it first.

Backpack

Map

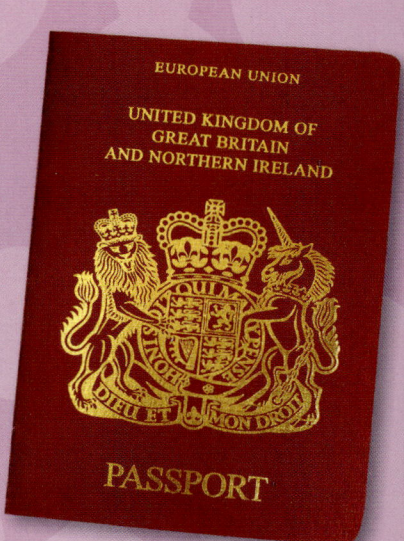

Tickets

Passport

Compass

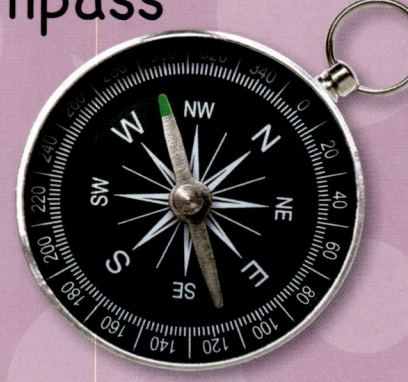

Suitcase

What to pack

Let's see, what do you need to pack for the trip?

Trousers

Swimming Goggles

Jacket

Sun Hat

Shirt

Sun Cream

Sandals

Sunglasses

Sweater

Shorts

Swimsuit

At the beach

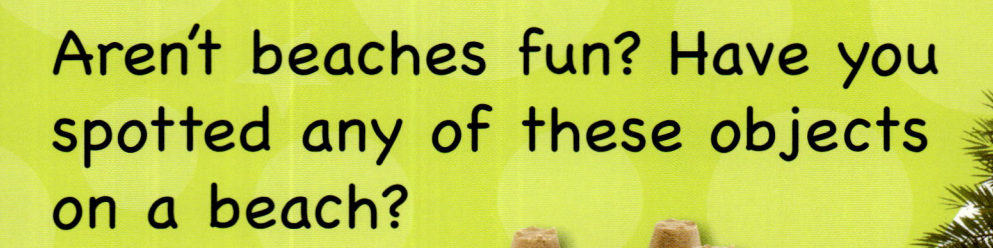

Aren't beaches fun? Have you spotted any of these objects on a beach?

Sandcastle

Palm Tree

Lifejacket

Surfboard

Shell

Bucket

Starfish

Hammock

- Frisbee
- Seashell
- Coral
- Dolphin
- Lifebuoy
- Beach Umbrella
- Deck Chair
- Crab
- Spade

Christmas

Yay, it's Christmas time!
Time for some holiday cheer.

Turkey

Bells

Hot Chocolate

Candles

Santa Claus

Cake

Present

Angel

Cookies

Christmas Stocking

Stars

Nativity

Sleigh

Tinsel

Holly

Holly Wreath

Reindeer

- Fireplace
- Cracker
- Christmas Hat
- Mistletoe
- Gingerbread Men
- Christmas Card
- Red Ribbon
- Christmas Tree
- Candy Cane
- Carol Singers

Snowman

Christmas Decorations

Elf

Eggnog

Lights

Family

Chimney

Halloween

Shhh...it's halloween. All the ghosts and spirits are about.

Candy

Scarecrow

Costumes

Bonfire

Skeleton

Ghost

Pumpkin Pie

Incense

Broomstick

Vampire

Bat

Mummy

Fireworks

Autumn Leaves

Witch

Pumpkin

Easter

Easter is not just about the egg hunt, is it?

Jellybean

Chocolate

Basket

Easter Bunny

Easter Eggs

Scones

Bonnet

Day out

How about a day of fun out with the other kids?

Swimming Pool

Binoculars

Pinecone

Treehouse

Tent

Camera

Windmill

Pebbles

Amusement park

Thrilling rides make a day at the amusement park.

Toy Car

Carousel

Sky Balloon Ride

Chair-O-Planes

Skittles

Go-kart

Roller Coaster

Boat Ride

Water Slide

Whirligig

Bumper Car

Ticket Booth

Spring Horse

Kiddie Train

Candy Floss

Ferris Wheel

In the kitchen

How many of these objects have you seen in your kitchen?

Blender

Sandwich Press

Microwave

Fridge

Oven

Toaster

Kettle

Kitchen Scales

Frying Pan

Food Containers

Knife

Baking Tray

Cutting Board

Rolling Pin

Dishwasher

Juicer

Ladle

In the study

The study is where people do their work.

Desk

Crayons

Pencil

Sharpener

Computer

Eraser

Desk Calendar

Ruler

- Armchair
- Pen
- Pen Stand
- Hole Punch
- Notebook
- Bookshelf
- Box File
- Stapler

In the dining room

You may find all these objects in the room where you have your meals.

Bananas

Fork

Pear

Apple

Strawberries

Butter

Cake

Orange

Table Mats

Plate

Yoghurt

Soup bowls

Salt and Pepper Shakers

Napkin Ring

Wine Glass

Napkin Holder

Napkin

In the garden

Do you have a garden? Have you seen these objects there before?

Plant

Watering Can

Flowerpot

Wheelbarrow

Gardening Gloves

Garden Chair

Gardening Shears

Spade

Clippers

Rake

Paving Stones

Flower

Trowel

Strimmer

Tree

Trowel

Fertiliser

Early vehicles

These are some of the earliest forms of transport used by man.

Longboat

Stagecoach

Sedan Chair

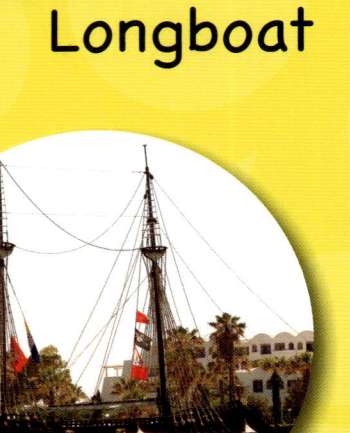

Galley

Buckboard

Covered Wagon

Buggy

Hansom Cab

Two wheelers

The bicycle is not the only machine on two wheels.

Super Bike

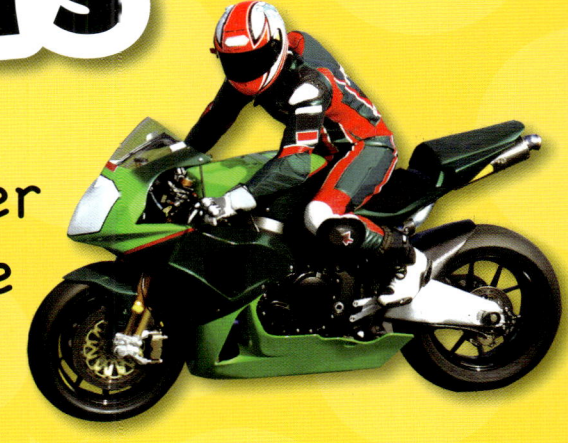

Cruiser Motorcycle

Scooter

Touring Bike

Moped

Bicycle

Dirt Bike

Street Motorcycle

Cars

There are so many different types of cars.

Go-kart

Limousine

Estate

Sports Car

4x4 Limousine

Racing Car

4x4

Hatchback Car

- Convertible
- Dragster
- Saloon
- Golf Buggy
- Vintage Car
- Mini Car
- Dune Buggy
- Minibus
- Jeep

Working machines

These machines are used to do different types of work.

Farm Tractor

Combine Harvester

Steamroller

Taxi

Forklift

Bulldozer

Ambulance

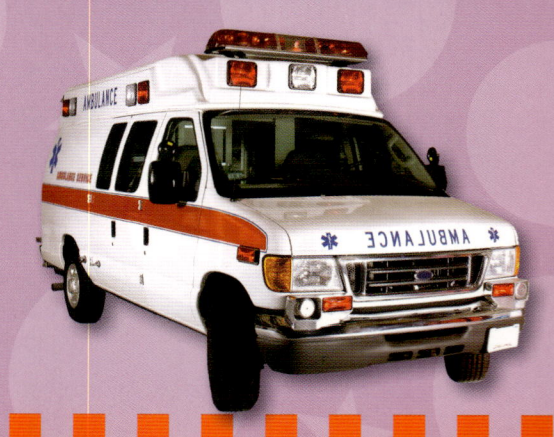

Rock Grader

Airport Tow Tractor

Digger

Fire Engine

Police Car

Baggage Train Tractor

Horse and Coach

Lawn Mower

Rubbish Truck

Delivery Van

Trucks & Buses

Have you ever seen so many different kinds of trucks and buses?

Cement Truck

Flatbed Truck

Dump Truck

Car Transporter

Articulated Lorry

Road Train

Tanker Truck

Mining Truck

Tow Truck

Coach

Motor Home

Pickup Truck

Monster Truck

Mini Truck

Trailer Truck

Double Decker Bus

Delivery Truck

Watercrafts

All these machines move on or below the water.

Cruise Ship

Hovercraft

Kayak

Cargo Ship

Life Raft

Barge

Canoe

Tanker Ship

Rowboat

Submarine

Motorboat

Sailboard

Race Boat

Luxury Boat

Catamaran

Sailboat

Hydrofoil

Aircrafts

High in the sky, that is where you will find these machines.

Glider

Attack Helicopter

Blimp

Passenger Plane

Radar Plane

Bomber

Tanker Plane

Hot Air Balloon

Passenger Helicopter

Small Plane

Cargo Plane

Sea Plane

Unmanned Drone

Biplane

Fighter Plane

Flying Boat

Hang Glider

Other vehicles

These machines are all different from the others. Can you tell why?

Snowmobile

Rickshaw

Train Engine

Space Shuttle

Tricycle

Autorickshaw

Segway

- Amphibious Vehicle
- Pram
- Monorail
- Skateboard
- Scooter
- Quadbike
- Sledge
- Rocket
- Tram
- Jet Ski

How I feel

We all have feelings and express them all the time.

Blushing

Wink

Excited

Surprised

Bored

Happy

Shy

Upset

Lonely

Playful

Sad

Angry

Scared

Tired

Teary

Hurt

Scowl

Musical instruments

Everybody loves music. Listening to music is a soothing experience.

Flute

Thumb Piano

Harmonica

Accordion

Tambourine

Mandolin

Drums

Indian Tabla Drums

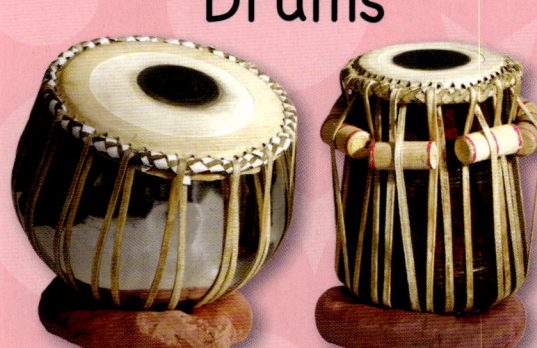

Saxophone

Maracas

Clarinet

Violin

Acoustic Guitar

Banjo

Piano

Ocarina

Carved African Djembe

Sports

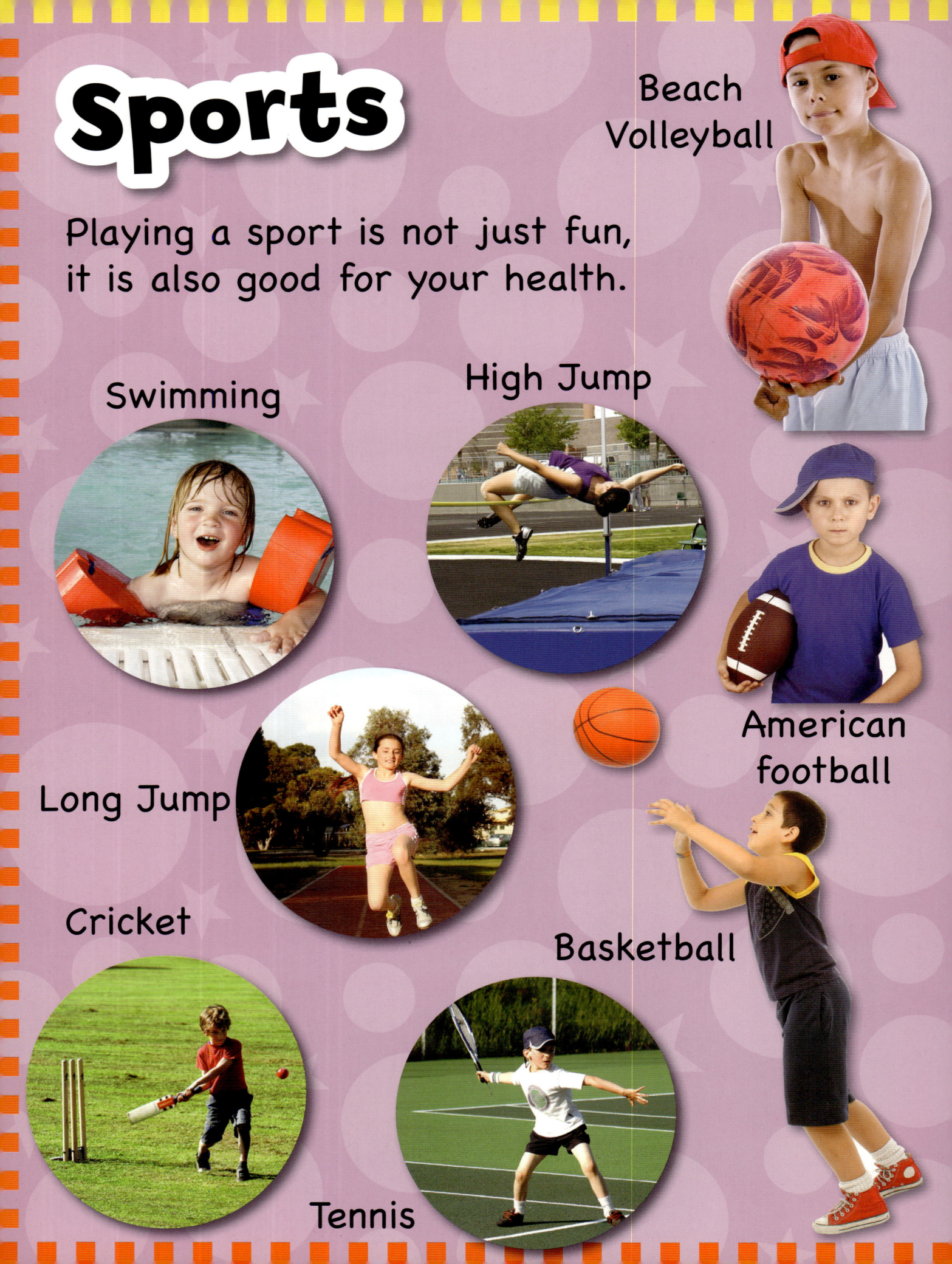

Playing a sport is not just fun, it is also good for your health.

Beach Volleyball

Swimming

High Jump

Long Jump

American football

Cricket

Basketball

Tennis

Football

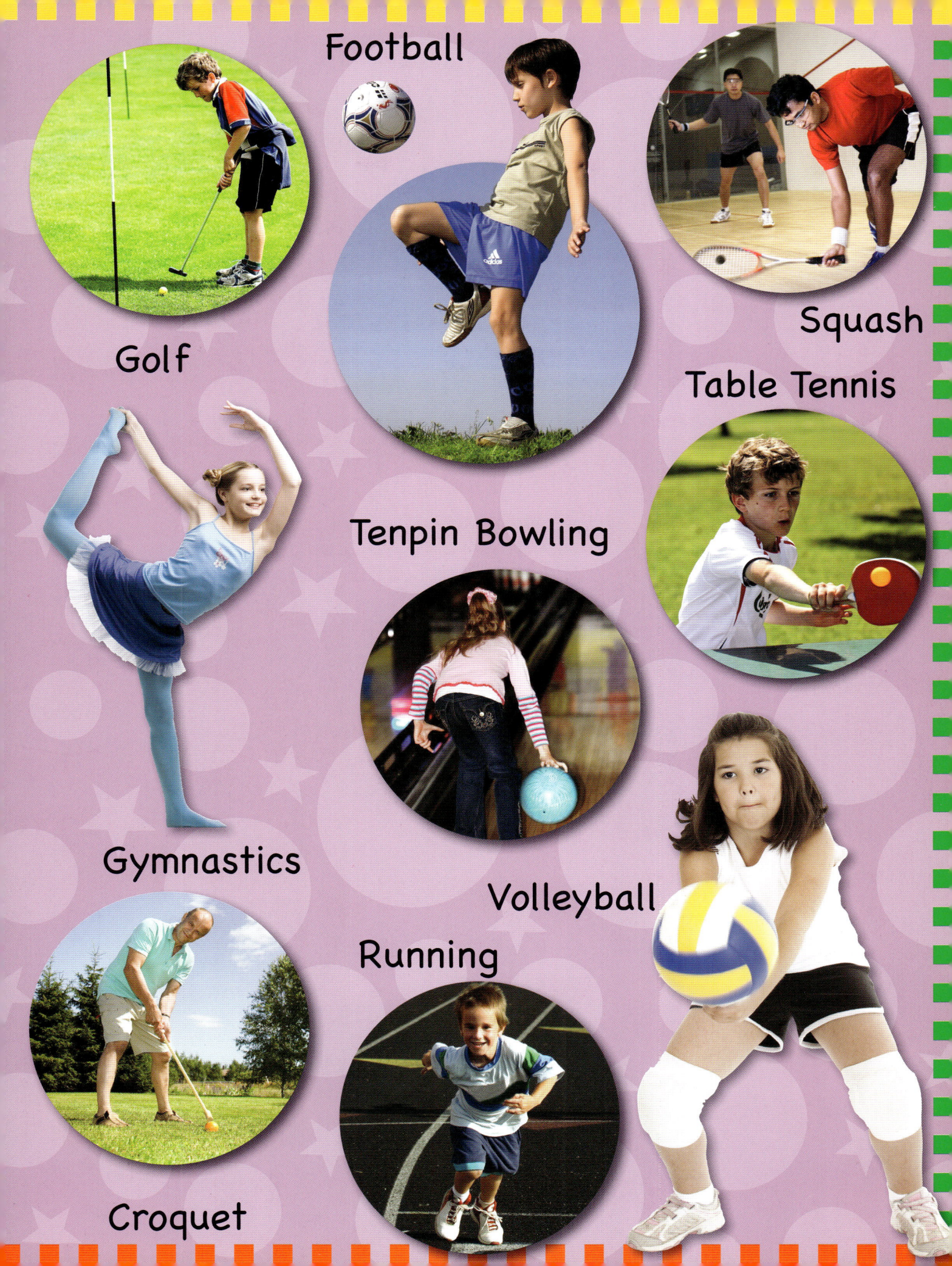

Squash

Golf

Table Tennis

Tenpin Bowling

Gymnastics

Volleyball

Running

Croquet

Games we play

And now it's time for some fun and games with friends.

Follow the Leader

Pat a Cake

Skipping

Cowboys and Indians

Backgammon

Draughts

Jigsaw Puzzles

Hopscotch

Chess

Hide and Seek

Frisbee

Rock Paper Scissors

Tag

Noughts & Crosses

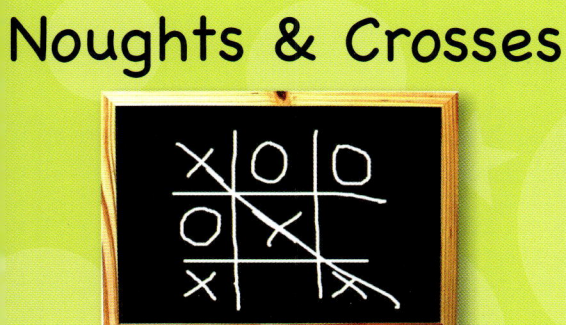

Marbles

Leapfrog

Catch

Descriptive words

These words tell you what something looks or feels like.

Soft

Small

Hard

Big

Hot

Cold

Short

Tall

Straight

Wide

Narrow

Bright

Weak

Dirty

Thin

Strong

Fat

In the school

These objects you may find in your school.

Cafeteria

Locker

Paintbrush

Teacher

Schooldesk

Schoolbag

- Flipchart
- Lunch Box
- Dustbin
- Notice Board
- Notebook
- Textbooks
- Water Bottle
- Globe
- Chalk
- Blackboard

Clothing accessories

Accessories are used with clothes and help us look good.

String Tie

Handbag

Tie Pin

Necktie

Mirror

Cufflinks

Wrist Watch

Coin Purse

Bow Tie

Hair Brush

Spectacles

Hairband

Neckerchief

Barrette

Umbrella

Ribbon

Wallet

Fruits

Everybody loves fruits, they are so juicy and delicious.

Cherry

Pineapple

Melon

Grape

Peach

Raspberry

Grapefruit

Blueberry

Plum

Fig

Watermelon

Kiwi

Guava

Mango

Lemon

Pomegranate

Papaya

Apricot

Vegetables

Vegetables are good for health. You should eat your vegetables.

Courgette

Carrot

Cabbage

Turnip

Spinach

Asparagus

Bell pepper

Broccoli

Celery

Peas

Radish

Lettuce

Cauliflower

Beetroot

Onion

Potato

Spices we use

Food tastes good when we add spices to give it flavour.

Coriander

Paprika

Star Anise

Fennel

Cardamom

Cloves

Mint

- Oregano
- Ginger
- Salt
- Bay Leaves
- Sage
- Garlic
- Nutmeg
- Black Pepper
- Saffron
- Parsley

Confectionary I eat

Do you have a sweet tooth? Then you will love these sweets.

Mousse

Cupcake

Pie

Lollipop

Meringues

Jelly

Fudge

Fruit Tart

Sweet Butter Fudge

Custard

Jelly Beans

Swiss Roll

Macaroons

Brownie

Crème Brûlée

Profiteroles

Sweets

Drinks

What do you like to drink on a hot day? Do you like these drinks?

Cola

Cranberry Juice

Buttermilk

Apple Juice

Iced Coffee

Water

Smoothie

Lemonade	Ginger Ale	Orange Juice
Tomato Juice	Milk Shake	Carrot Juice
Coffee		Hot Chocolate
Tea	Iced Tea	

Foods I eat

What is your favourite food?
Do you like any of these?

Fajita

Sushi

Pasta

Soup

Hamburger

Corn-on-the-cob

Meatloaf

Pancakes

Lasagna

Taco

Salad

Fish and Chips

Bacon Roll

Curry

Pizza

Fried Rice

Steak

Snacks

Feeling hungry? How about a tasty snack?

Bagel

Chips

Croissant

Crackers

Energy Bar

Doughnuts

Hot Dog

Sandwich

Nachos

Pretzel

Nuts

Quiche

Waffles

Marshmallows

Raisins

Wafers

Popcorn

Condiments

These products help make our food taste better. Ketchup anyone?

Pickle

Honey

Vinegar

Salad Dressing

Ketchup

Olive Oil

Soy Sauce

- Jam
- Chilli Sauce
- Chocolate Sauce
- Mustard
- Marmalade
- Sour Cream
- Mayonnaise
- Barbeque Sauce
- Cheese Spread
- Salsa

Flowers

Everybody loves flowers. They are so colourful and sweet smelling.

Lotus

Rose

Forget-Me-Not

Foxglove

Lilly

Chrysanthemum

Sunflower

	Tulip	
Daffodil		Primrose

Orchid

Bird of Paradise

Iris

Dahlia

Daisy

Crocus

People I meet

How many of these people have you met lately?

Blacksmith

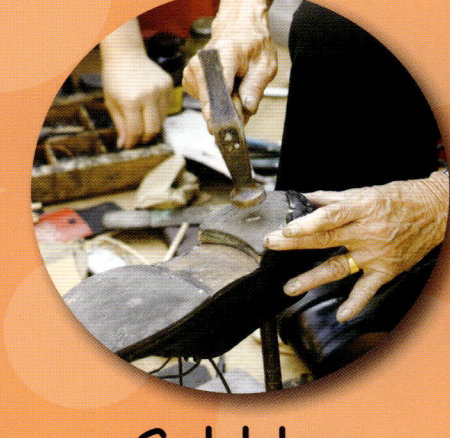

Doctor

Fisherman

Cobbler

Carpenter

Fireman

Engineer

- Farmer
- Astronaut
- Hair Dresser
- Doorman
- Chef
- Bellboy
- Greengrocer
- Butler
- Chauffeur

Lifeguard

Lawyer

Sailor

Soldier

Painter

Archeologist

Newspaper Girl

Pilot

Nurse

Tailor

Postman

Sculptor

Maid

Electrician

Security guard

Builder

Priest

Beautician

Places I go

These are some of the places you may visit for different reasons.

Cinema

Shopping Centre

Amusement Park

School

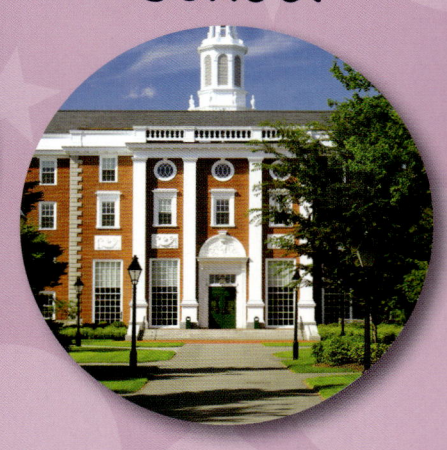

Bookshop

Greengrocer

Library

Restaurant

Delicatessen

Swimming Pool

Park

Arcade

Laundrette

Zoo

Museum

Toy Shop

Clothes Shop

Story Characters

What are your favourite characters? What do you like reading about?

Castle

Prince

Magician

King

Monster

Dragon

Princess

Mermaid

Wizard

Troll

Unicorn

Pony

Fairy

Ballerina

Knight

Red Indian

Things to do

How many of these activities do you do?

Lie Down

Hug

Dance

Shout

Sit

Drive

Shake Hands

Run

- Play Fight
- Whisper
- Sing
- Kick
- Kiss
- Walk
- Wave
- Stand
- Push

My tools

These are some of the tools your parents might use around the house.

Hammer

Saw

Nuts

Hacksaw

Measuring Tape

Scissors

- Wrench
- Nails
- Chisel
- Needle
- Spanner
- Crowbar
- Drill
- Wire Cutter
- Pliers
- Screwdriver
- File

Baby animals

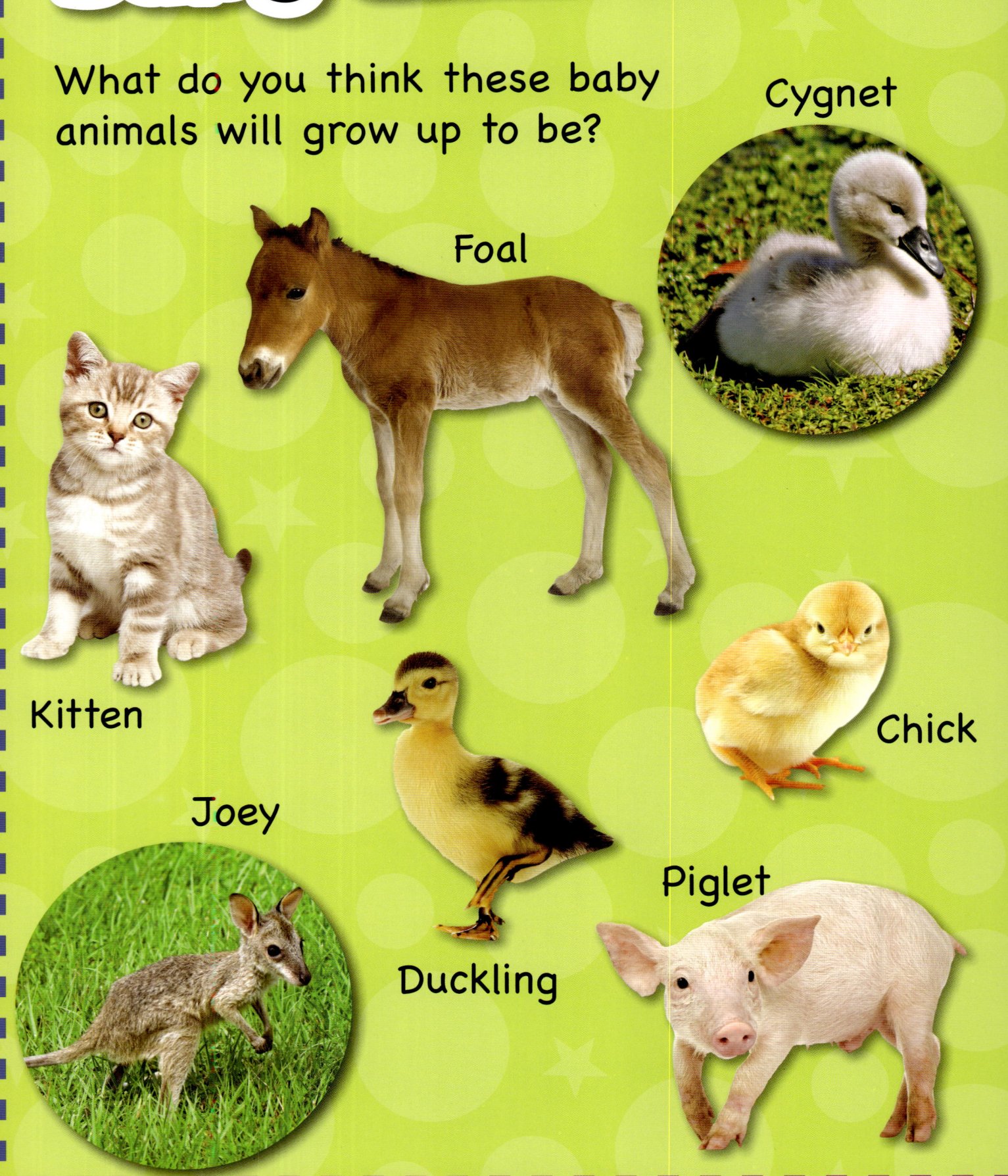

What do you think these baby animals will grow up to be?

Cygnet

Foal

Kitten

Joey

Duckling

Chick

Piglet

Kid

Puppy

Lion Cub

Calf

Fawn

Lamb

Tadpole

Alligator Hatchling

Rabbit Kit

Gosling

Valuables

All these things are precious and expensive. Be careful with them.

Coins

Coral

Emerald

Opal

Garnet

Gold

Pearl

Amber

Currency Notes

Platinum

Silver

Diamond

Turquoise

Ruby

Jade

Topaz

Sapphire

Jewellery

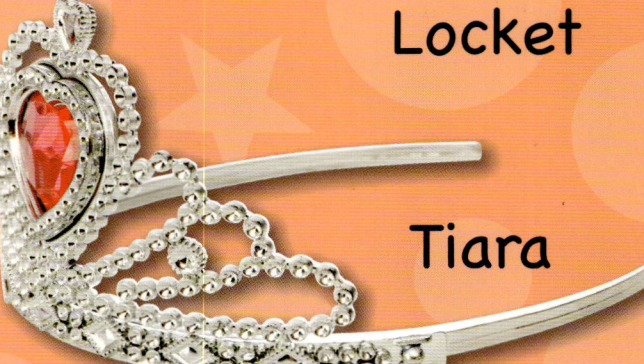

Lots of women wear jewellery.

Necklace

Earring

Pendant

Anklet

Hair Clip

Locket

Tiara

- Bracelet
- Amulet
- Brooch
- Hair Pin
- Bangle
- Hair Sticks
- Ring
- Toe Ring
- Choker

Shapes

These are some of the common shapes you will find around you.

Cylinder

Spiral

Triangle

Diamond

Cone

Crescent

Star

Circle

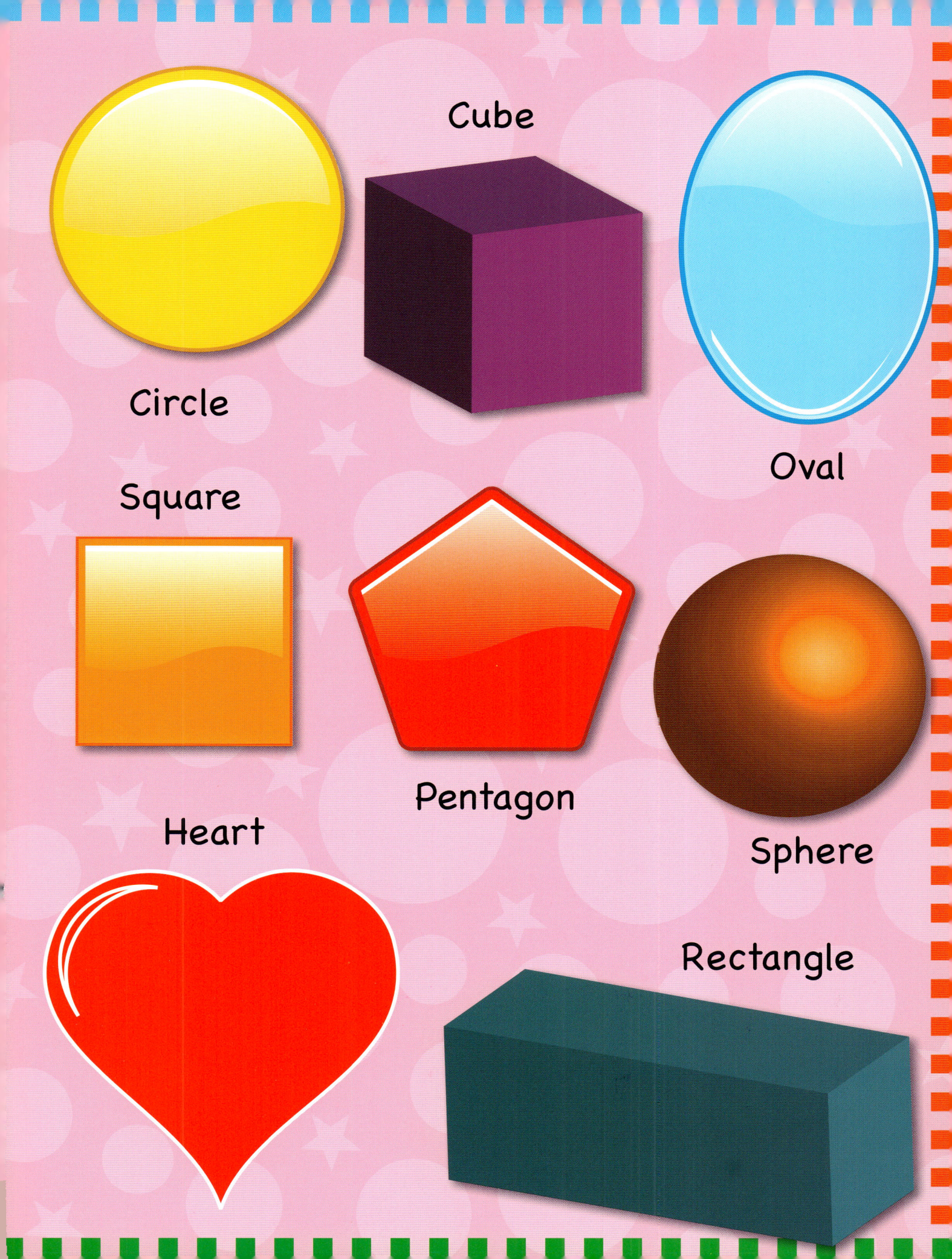

Cube

Oval

Square

Pentagon

Sphere

Heart

Rectangle